THE WAIVER OF THE ILLEGAL ALIENS: ANARCHY OR JUSTICE

THE WAIVER OF THE ILLEGAL ALIENS: ANARCHY OR JUSTICE

Hugo Aguilera

Library of Congress Control Number: 2014960316
ISBN: Hardcover   978-1-4633-9789-0
                 Softcover   978-1-4633-9788-3
                 eBook   978-1-4633-9787-6

Print information available on the last page.

Rev. date: 25/08/2015

To order additional copies of this book, contact:
Palibrio
1663 Liberty Drive, Suite 200
Bloomington, IN 47403
Toll Free from the U.S.A 877.407.5847
Toll Free from Mexico 01.800.288.2243
Toll Free from Spain 900.866.949
From other International locations +1.812.671.9757
Fax: 01.812.355.1576
orders@palibrio.com
699580

TABLE OF CONTENTS

Introduction vii

Foreword ix

CHAPTER 1. Choosing the Theatre 1

CHAPTER 2. The Turmoil 3

CHAPTER 3. Prohibited Entrances 5

CHAPTER 4. Order Restitution 9

SECOND PART
THE METAPHOR'S INTERPRETATION

CHAPTER 5. Which one is the Main Door? 15

CHAPTER 6. Illegal Entrance 19

CHAPTER 7. The Dilemma of the Undocumented: Anarchy or Justice ... 23

THIRD PART
NEGLECTED ARGUMENTS

CHAPTER 8. Causes that Motivate Migration 27

CHAPTER 9. When Migration is Dangerous 33

CHAPTER 10. Beneficiaries of Illegal Immigration 37

CHAPTER 11. USA: An Empire with Severe Risks of Falling 43

INTRODUCTION

The authorities of the United States; such as Congress, the Senate and the President of the United States of America will determine the fate of several million immigrants who find themselves illegally in the United States as well as another million who have been awaiting for many years; hoping the obtain the precious immigrant visa for the United States of America.

The vast majority in this country either ignores or does not care to know what may happen with an uncontrollable migration in this present time. It is advisable to take into account what a missionary, head of the Catholic Church) once said over twenty years ago: "Protestant countries are the trashcan of the Catholic Church".

FOREWORD

Four Democratic senators and four Republican senators concluded on April 15, 2104 that a waiver would permit the pardon of eleven million undocumented immigrants currently living in the United States. The reason or motive as to why **they are given this constitutional grace has not been explained**; however, this is permitted by **Presidential Decreed**; in addition, **it is also an important reason for Presidential Elections**.

What the Senate committee ignores is that surely that same day a new process without any agreed deadline, which will repeat the regularization of the other X millions of undocumented immigrants will be starting and will form **the THIRD AMNESTY thereby writing a new never ending story**.

CHAPTER 1

Choosing the Theatre

In a quiet village in the East Coast of the United States, where daily life is full of pleasant tranquility and a calm peace can be inhaled, (a peace wished for in many regions of the world where violence and social animosity prevail) a theater company capriciously agreed to present a highly sought theatrical play in a medium size theater, which will leave out a high number of followers. This, of course, was consciously done.

CHAPTER 2

The Turmoil

Hours before the show, the interested crowd started to gather and the inevitable happened: The high number of people who wanted to enjoy the play at all cost, brought chaos to the main entrance; however, the turmoil of the people who wanted to pay to see the show, was the least of the problems that arise.

CHAPTER 3

Prohibited Entrances

There were also other people who wanted to enter through the emergency exit door, which is a prohibited entrance. These were a group of friends of the security guard in charge of this exit door, who were able to sneak in because of their relationship with the security guard or by paying a modest fee. When the chaos was at its climax, the security guard decided to block the emergency exit door and a third group of people angered by the security's guard unfairness, and rejection opted to enter by force by breaking the window located a few meters away from the emergency exit door of the building. By this time the security guard was unable to react to the illegal trespassing of this people, because of his unethical behavior when letting his friends in. As a result, people who did not pay ended inside the theater crowding the corridors and stairways.

In the meantime, outside the theater were people who deserved to get in, but couldn't because by the time that a report from the people in charge was made the theater was completely full, due to the irregularities and poor planning of the theater management and its bad security.

Due to these circumstances, informational reports made by the different departments could not be analyzed with care and time, a decision needed to be made immediately as to how to resolve the chaos at hand.

On the one side, there was dissatisfaction from the customers that had paid for their tickets, expecting to view a great, enjoyable show under comfortable conditions; however, the overbooking that saturated the environment with unwanted odors made them very uncomfortable. On the other side, the amount of income expected by the administration was greatly diminished because of the large amount of people that came in without paying, while outside were people willing to pay for the tickets up to three times its value.

A report made by the maintenance employees presented damages to the building made by the vandalism of the people that violently broke their entrance to the theater.

The security cameras detected some of the faces, and the security department awaited for instruction to proceed in calling the police department, and look for the identified individuals before the last call which will initiate the show.

This report was placed on top of the desk of the General Manager of the Theater, and also in his office were the organizers of the show and the theater owners to determine the most convenient resolution.

Due to the time constraints to make a decision, the following actions were proposed:

A) Suspension of the show, and ticket refund to all who presented their receipt.

B) Suspension of the show until the next day, and a requirement to present a receipt in order to enter the show the next day.

C) Exit all people through the emergency door, and bring them back thru the front door, escorted by the police, with the requirement to show their receipt in order to enter. Whoever does not have a ticket should be sanctioned; and those identified as trespassers will be charged in accordance with their acts.

D) Let everyone watch the show at once in order to keep everyone happy since everyone is already inside; and, the insurance can pay for all damages.

The General Manager with a discerning attitude takes the documents and takes refuge in the private annex room to think over the situation and decide on the most convenient way to handle it.

CHAPTER 4

Order Restitution

After a couple of minutes, he walks back into his office and presents before the people awaiting the solution, which he thought, was the best way to solve the problem at hand. He started by saying:

First of all, call the police, it will be needed, when they arrive, place them in front of the exit door of the theater, where the security guard's friends and the security guard entered, **the one who sparked this disorder**. Secondly, **management will announce by microphone the first call to see the show**, asking the people sitting at the hallways and stairs to follow the instructions that will be given to them by the service and security personnel, with the help of some police men to go to the Lobby of the theater. Once they start moving into the Lobby, the Security Chief, will request for all personnel to have their ticket on hand, and those who in fact have a ticket will enter the Lobby, and those who do not have a ticket will be directed to another exit door, where the police will be waiting for them. Among this people will be the ones who broke the glass windows.

Once this part of the operation concludes, management will announce the second call to watch the show, asking people already sitting at the main show room to present their entrance ticket to the theater security personnel. If there is someone who has lost their entrance ticket, this persons will accompany the theater security personnel to be assigned a seat; however, the cahiers that sold the tickets will be awaiting behind the glass window to identify the people whom they did or did not sell tickets to, and asking the security personnel to escort them back to their seat if identified.

The leftover people whom did not reach the Lobby will be divided between the ones that paid with credit card and the ones that gave another type of payment. Lastly, in order to avoid any kind of injustice, a sheet with five alleged cashier pictures, that were supposedly selling the tickets, will be shown to the rest of the people. Obviously, the ones who identify the cashiers are the ones that never bought a ticket and these persons will be taken to the emergency exit to be integrated with the rest who did not pay a ticket. The people who did not identify the alleged cashiers who supposedly sold the tickets will be return to the inside of the theater. The people that are seating already and showed their ticket must be counted and will be compared with the number of tickets sold, the difference between both will be given to the ones that lost their ticket, and the leftovers are the trespassers that came in through the window. After this last process, management will make the last call which will instruct everyone that the show is about to begin.

I hope this proposal is accepted by everyone; however, if there is a better solution I am willing to listen to it.

After everyone in his office was convinced that this was the best way to solve the problem, they stepped out of the office with the conviction that they will be observing the development of this situation to intervene only if necessary.

One of the organizers told one of the owners, that he was very intrigued by a comment that the General Manager had made to him before presenting his strategy. He said that he felt that the same thing happens to President Obama, and he wanted to see if the General Manager could clarify this comment. The owner responded that he agreed, because he was also intrigued by this comment and when he was ready to clarify it, he would also be present. They both left looking for the General Manager to make his explanation.

SECOND PART

THE METAPHOR'S INTERPRETATION

CHAPTER 5

Which one is the Main Door?

After the situation was in order and the abusive trespassers were taken to the proper authorities, the organizers and owners requested an explanation from the General Manager as to the similarity of what just happened at the theater, with the situation developing with the regularization that President Barack Obama was about to sign.

The General Manager said that the **Obama's dilemma** was: who to regulate.

The facts established by narrating the theater situation facilitates, and simplifies the understanding of the problem, because it allows to locate the main characters involved in the unaccepted illegal immigration, which is very common in the United States, and is surprisingly seen as an everyday act of daily life.

When I was obligated by the situation to separate the legal participants from the illegal ones, I figured out the following:

The theater is the United States territory.

The show is the Legal Residence known as the "Green Card".

The General Manager is President Barrack Obama.

The owners of the theater are The House of Representatives.

The promoters are The Senate.

The main entrance to the theater is the authorized entrance to the United States, such as International Bridges, Airports, Seaports, etc., through which people that seek legal entrance show their permits and legal documents to enter, or start a legal process of entry, respecting the laws, regulations and conditions imposed by the United States authority with diverse documents, depending on the specified situation. Some of these

processes are resolved in a very short time, while others take years to be approved, and here lays the vast majority of people aspiring to be residents who are displaced by the "steamed" regularization of the illegal.

CHAPTER 6

Illegal Entrance

The emergency exit door represents all the places where inspections take place in the United States through where undocumented immigrants present fake documents, and are let in by the authorities because of their complicity; also, concealment of people in vehicles through bridges and checkpoints, and all activities involving corruption in which the authorities are also involved at the time that undocumented immigrants enter the country. This modus operandi took place massively when President Jimmy Carter granted an exemption which resulted in the first chain link that does not permit Republicans to reach the White House because of all the millions that now form a vast number of corporate votes in favor of Democrats in appreciation for the effortless processes given to obtain the legal residence at that time. **This shameful act of deception and breach of immigration laws presented him as a winner of the Nobel Peace Prize.** Many millions benefited from apocryphal documents and this act of corruption encumbered democrats to own permanency of the Presidency since those times accompanied by elements of low moral character.

Another illegal entrance is the glass window where people entered violently causing much damage to the theater: this entry represents individuals that enter through rivers, boundary markers, gap borders, deserts and all places not authorized for entry with or without help from those already occupying the United States territory. It is this category that holds a greater number of criminals, rapists, and law breakers that receive assistance from the Mexican side without identifying the type of the individual's qualities which shows poor appreciation of having good relations between countries. **As is the case of the Catholic Church, one of the main promoters of the illegal entry of immigrants to the United States that seeks to increase their membership and power to become the official church of the state by providing corporate votes of**

appreciation to the ranks of the Democratic Party in its fight to obtain legal or illegal residence. It is worth to mention that the country where the headquarters of the Catholic Church are established is Italy, where illegal immigration is punished by incarceration and deportation, contrary to what is solicited from the United States.

The question that must be brought up is: **Does the authorities of the United States of America, defenders of Liberty and Justice possess in illegal immigration a fortunate opportunity to win the good battle for justice?** Of course not, rather the presented behavior seems to mimic an anarchist regime that despises law and rewards those who violate it. It practices an amendment which is obsolete in its proceedings. Is this why Representatives, Senators, the President, and Judges are being paid for, to be shameful of their laws by giving reason to anarchy?

CHAPTER 7

The Dilemma of the Undocumented: Anarchy or Justice

Under this erratic fashion are designed most of the resolutions issued by the Senate in the last several years, with social answers without proper explanation, placing the future of the United States in a plummet where there is no moving forward and forming a never ending story.

It hasn't been that long that the United States want to pull out of Iraq, and the authorities are already thinking of going to Korea. The US supports Palestinians, and is also ally of the Israelites. The US authorities give amnesty to 11 million undocumented immigrants residing inside the country, and thirty years ago the same process was enacted during the times of Jimmy Carter, executioner of the Venezuelan people, and a door was opened to the third amnesty benefiting the undocumented immigrants that came in after April 15 of 2013.

Korea, Cuba, Israel, Afghanistan, Iraq ... as if the Senate was an imitation of the United Nations its decision making occupies the air of undefined rarities.

THIRD PART

NEGLECTED ARGUMENTS

CHAPTER 8

Causes that Motivate Migration

The migration phenomena occur for various reasons, natural disasters such as droughts and floods, extreme poverty which is raised as if by natural order, and others which are of a social order such as civil wars, world wars or even political reasons, where ethnic groups are displaced when rival groups take control of their regions and they are forced to migrate. Overpopulation is also a reason. Religion, which plants migration because of the professing of different creeds, and the religious leaders who try to impose their Faith by obligation, an act strongly criticized of the Catholic and Muslim religion considered intolerant religions which integrate special groups to perform these negative actions in which the Jesuits order is found who was in charge of the "Holy" inquisition lead by the feared Ignacio de Loyola. This character persecuted harshly, up to the coast of the Netherlands in front of the British Islands, the groups of pioneers who founded the first American Colonies, which served as the melting pot where the foundation of the country called United States of America was cultivated.

This historical fact is nothing alike to what "other" denominations of Protestants conceptualized, among which are found the reformed Catholics, Baptists, etc., that erroneously part from the **1700's instead of what happened during 1610**, when it was defined for the first time what the "American Dream" meant: A better life of comfort and tranquility, full of bonuses and food stamps which permit people to work less and take it easy, an even have many kids to be able to live of the government. Customs being practiced professionally by the youth in today's society. Youth which bears children every year and keep their spouse pregnant with the following one, while the suffering soldiers, **AUTHENTIC HEROES** of this country, are left disabled by fighting for the **nation's best reasons**, and who are found writing letters to ask for two cents, to help them fight their permanent disability. **Is this a case of ingratitude?**

Two historical migrations that have powerfully influenced in the global arena are the one from Israel and the one from the United States, where their greatness was written before its foundation through prophecies which have become real as if part of universal history.

The one form Israel call for our attention because of its ancient character, which remains present and on its way to Armageddon, while the empires that controlled it are extinct.

The Assyrian Empire, Chaldeans, Babylonians, Romans, Ottomans, the Catholic Inquisition, Nazis and others which ordered its annihilation and persecution have disappeared or remain in the darkness of evil waiting for its return, waiting for deadly vengeance; however, Israel by God's biblical decreed remains in force and keeps looking for its divine inheritance. This comment I make in a way that it becomes an accelerator of events because from the UN itself, this events of destruction might take place. **Try it, practice it, order it, but you will not be able to destroy the people of our Lord Jesus Christ; you will not be able to.**

Likewise, the United States was directly appointed by the Apostle John in the book of Apocalypses, in the visions of Nostradamus, and by Pastor Robinson who envisioned the Netherland ships that would establish the new Amsterdam, which is today New York, by persecuted

Christians **called Puritans by the English Episcopal**, who established **the colonies that gave origin to the United States of America.**

Why is it that educational institutions try to ignore something so obvious in history? Unfortunately in the scholastic course of the history of schools from Elementary to University events have gone unnoticed which obligated the English to take the determination to propose to the Puritans a trip to this distant land full of savages and tribes that not even the English or French army could subdue. The attack strategies used by these natives consisted of ambushes used on the guerrilla and in both armies, which consisted of fighting on an open field without any kind of protection, but patriotic valor.

The strategy consisted on the Puritans being escorted from behind at a distance by the army, while waiting for the Indians to come out, becoming a visible target for the Army's artillery.

The skills of the Indians who knew the terrain, permitted them to evade this and at the same time managed to capture many of the Puritans, whom unarmed, where an easy prey for the terrible warriors. That is where the promise begins and with the protection of our Lord Jesus Christ, just as the protection given to the Great Moses before the Pharaoh through the gifts which he shared between men. One of these gifts we find the discernment of spirits, a valuable tool of the Biblical God that permitted the Indians to be respected, when tied by their hands and just about to be sacrificed to the fire, before **imminent death**, they called their captors and with the also the gift of tongue, in the captor's dialect, they inculcated to them a vast number of medical prescriptions due to their captors illnesses. This was communicated from their prison, without even seeing the sick, they knew what illnesses they suffered.

Amazed by what they saw, when they untied their hands and anointed them with the anointing oil, this Indians were called "witches". Within their social environment, this title gave them magic characteristics, **accompanied by great respect.**

Under these conditions, the evangelization of Mohicans, Sioux and many types of tribes which were disseminated through those abrupt regions of the North of the United States and South of Canada, began. It was not the Englishman who assisted, it was their task; however, to place them in the right place, where their mission was to begin. It was actually the power of the living and true God who **made the miracle of Colonization, and for this reason, this country is a land of promises, not of anarchism or fundamentals of a better life. Its purpose and goals are of a greater wingspan,** not of reasons to waste time by making inane laws which show the insecurity of not knowing what to do, at the time that a historical event is happening.

Wasting time by messing up even more the rare future of ten million of unemployed, who demand urgent work sources, and to analyze how to regulate **millions of undocumented**, which will complicate even more the labor issue, calls for the analysis of this persons whom immediately need psychological treatment in which it will be shown that when there are 10 leftovers, the answer is not to add eleven undocumented, which throws overboard all the process made by the financial and production efficiency by falling in the waters of inequality and the labor leadership of selfish and ambitious individuals, this situation can only be considered a waste of time, similar to the practices at the UN, where in the last few years success has not been achieved.

CHAPTER 9

When Migration is Dangerous

One of the most painful pages in the history of the United States is the sly way in which terrorist Arabs presented documents which identified them as future students of an aviation course, but in reality they were suicide activists that came with the malevolent purpose to destroy the Twin Towers of New York.

They entered through the south border of Mexico to avoid suspicion of any kind. Their purpose was well defined and they came to die for their own wrong reasons.

Just like these extremist, there are also individuals that enter this country seeking a better way of life, but who conceal their true purpose under the protection of an organized good intention of doing harm to this country. This exists because in the United States the word **promiscuity and ingenuity have no meaning in their dictionaries. Critics have used them under their own prejudice throughout the years, and have never obtained a proper answer to the fact that this two words are the center of national debate.**

The wickedness and the abuse to respect that should be granted to the President of the United States and to the citizens in general by those who have come here soliciting help and protection "plethoric of hope for a better life" etc. etc. after a little while, especially Latin American, long and want a similar life to what has been left behind at their distant land. **Thus, creating a ghost of nationality to which the United States cannot compete with because this patriotic feeling passes the United States citizenship to a second place equal to a necessary evil in order to live a better life by obtaining the benefits of US Citizenship, but** with great disrespect to what it represents.

At the UN is estimated that the offense to respect that must be given to the host country such as the United States, the abuse to the "law of Diplomatic Immunity" has superseded the boundaries that it should have, and on the contrary, it has reach rudeness towards the President, while this useless organization, creator of the imbalance that exists in the world today, has not sanction the ones whom without regard have expressed feelings of intolerance and contempt for this nation that seeks to mend the ruptures to international concordance.

Another lack of respect that has not been sanctioned and that should be is the freedom of expression made by anarchist disguised like social activist whom cynically enter the precincts that represent the legality of this country and fight without regard as if reason assisted them. Just as it happened at the undocumented marches through the different streets of the United States without the fulfillment of the obligations to which officials swear to when taking possession of their post, obligations such as to execute and enforce the laws of this country. This situation brings embarrassment to the image of the United States and to what it represents: principles of Legality and Justice even outside its territory. This damages are directly engaged to the military and civilians who are in charge of enforcing the fulfillment of the law within their country; however, it is not being done which creates an alliance with anarchist by opening legal causes to achieve their wrong intentions, and marks treachery to the country that they represent.

Mrs. Napolitano during a TV interview was interrupted by an individual who requested the stop to deportation of undocumented without due diligence, immediately Mrs. Napolitano associated herself to this petition **ignoring that the officers that execute deportations have the right and the legality to accomplish it; however, she disqualified them and created a common cause with the anarchist who asked for the law to be ignored, thus making Mrs. Napolitano an activist. This has been done by many of the politicians who are protected and seeking a Nobel Prize, but in her case it was to win popular sympathy, hearts and minds. In reality this act was an act of treason what she is and what she represents as others that have been given this prize have done.**

She is not the only official who has expressed anarchist behavior, there are many others, and it may be correct to say that the majority of state politicians do not want to accept their responsibilities; but they react as "butter on fire", when they are faced with dumb petitions without legal basis which motivate their manifestations, so this is the legal promiscuity that confuses citizens and public officials causing the loss of authority that validates their positions.

CHAPTER 10

Beneficiaries of Illegal Immigration

The beneficiaries of illegal immigration are:

The country of MEXICO, benefiting by the manpower workforce that sends remittances of money, which are considered the second national source of income after petroleum; moreover, the low educational standards will keep them being politically manipulated by the political systems in Mexico such as the **PRI** and in the United States the **Democratic Party**, main promoter of this **anarchist** attitude of illegal regularization.

The Roman Catholic Church which increases its members and economic resources through donations which translate to twenty two millions of dollars a week, considering that every legalized undocumented immigrant will provide at least twenty dollars per week through donations and considering that through the same medium during times of the dreamer Jimmy Carter, the amount was more less the same for this type of legalized residents; although, this amount could reach forty four million a week net income, which makes this church the richest in the world without having to pay a penny on taxes.

Fascist, whom have an existing agreement with the Catholic leadership, especially the Roman Catholic leadership headed by the Popes: Pio XII, Juan XXIII, Pablo VI, Juan Pablo I, Juan Pablo II, and the last two in force. It is probably considered that this seditious and criminal groups disappeared at the end of World War II, but this is entrusted sinning because we must take into account that after the trials of Nuremberg, Von Papen and the Papacy exited unharmed despite being highly involved in the brutal persecutions of the members of the resistance formed in Continental Europe, especially in France and the Netherlands, where thousands of citizens were brutally tortured and murdered because of the complaints they reported from the church to the bloodthirsty members of the dreaded SS Nazi of those countries and others.

The sympathy felt by the Kennedys and Franklin D. Roosevelt towards fascism, did not allow for punishment to the members of the Roman Catholic leadership, despite petitions by General **Charles De Gaulle and the 1**st **Prime Minister Winston Churchill** in Nuremberg. Ignored by Roosevelt and as if this wasn't enough he shared the world with the former partner of the Nazis, the communist and murdered **Jose Stalin**. To prove further and for the sake of confirmation that fascism exits inside the White House, later on during 1953 the Catholic Church signed an agreement with Adolf Hitler's godfather, the Spanish Jesuit dictator Francisco Franco, idol of Fidel Castro, the Cuban Dictator.

The **Democratic Party** is greatly benefited by the contingents that enter illegally into the United States, with the help of Mexico, the Catholic Church, and Fascists. A good part of these contingents, manage to obtain their citizenship, and this are guaranteed votes of "gratitude", since they are traditionalist idolaters. Their children who are being born in this country, who considered themselves Mexican, whom their documents grant them the privilege of being United States citizens, and therefore whether or not ignorant, their birth certificate will allow them at the age of eighteen to participate with "gratitude" votes in favor of the Democratic party, causing the Democratic race for subsequent years, to be flawed as in other countries, such as in Mexico, where the unions, the ignorant, the poor and the religious have the leadership of victory, and convert Democracy into Aristocracy, because the candidates will be elected by parties not by the people.

Supporters that the United Stated be a cosmopolitan country, before this crossroad the future of the United States will reach the so longed "change" that President Barrack Obama offered during his first campaign for the candidacy to President of the United Stated to accomplish what was said by the Dictator Adolf Hitler, that the United States was a country of black men and with the events that were taking place since the middle of the last century, the symbolic change of the United States will be to be Afro-Latin, their language English-Spanish and their main religion Roman Catholic with the great advantage that it will request to be the official religion of this unfortunate country if their present citizens allow it. Surely during the judgement of the Nations, the United Stated will have much to explain about this fact of being a chosen country for the Glory of God Our Lord Jesus Christ; however, ended up being a Catholic colony, immerse in idolatry and **bodyguard of the United Nations without pay or benefit.**

As a closing prayer it is necessary that the events arising from the United Stated soil with the awakening of the Citizens who love this country are accomplished with the help of our Lord Jesus Christ:

To end the unfortunate results that may occur in the immediate future, join efforts and build good deeds for the Lord, such as to investigate and ascertain limitations to be able to fix the redemption of the nation. **AMEN, AMEN and AMEN.**

CHAPTER 11

USA: An Empire with Severe Risks of Falling

From the depths of its own being, the United States is an empire which about a little more than a Century ago surprised their own and also strangers because if the way that it developed its powerful structure placing itself as the vanguard of the nations; influenced by its geopolitics for having coastlines towards the two great oceans, vast natural resources and the most convincing reason for its potential: The Genesis of its pioneer population, the melting pot of its home where it cooked up the citizenship of its first settlers called by the English as **The Puritans**.

Contrary to other migrations from the new continent, formed by military cams of unprepared people, thieves, adventurers, etc., the puritans were the pilgrims emerged from the coasts of Netherlands which carried contingents of people with a high degree of preparation, that came to the coasts of North America. Intellectuals such as college teachers, farmers, accountants, doctors, engineers, who formed the block of believers in the new teachings of the gospel and resisted and achieved to avoid the blaze of persecution practiced by the beneficiaries of Roger Williams, in its unfortunate application of freedom of cults, to enter with equal rights to the new country founded by the persecuted. Persecuted who did not give up in the midst of the unending planting of terror that sacrificed the heresy by fire to make them break their faith through fear. The pioneers, with sadness, saw the lives of many being consummated, lives of friends who professed the same faith that kept them bearing such disgrace to plant a seed of fear that did not grow. That in itself was the shield of faith that constructed the character of the pioneers. Is there any similitude with the modern pioneers?

Illegal immigrants by spiritual idolatry conviction in its vast majority, who demand without legal right or historical right and of pragmatic reasoning a residence

in the country founded by pilgrims who have nothing in common with them!!!!!

Under the umbrella of one of those hateful comparisons, if we analyze the present "United States Citizen", a description not given to the first settlers of this country, we might end up crying. Its principles, its dreams, its hopes are diametrically **opposites**. While the pioneers were not intimidated by the fire of the Holy Inquisition, clowns such as Castro and Chavez or the anarchist without social conscience, the so called terrorist that without a degree of tolerance result to be the same ones that were at the bonfire of old Europe, have present US Citizens on their toes full with fear.

While the pioneers without an Army, triumphed over the adversity of who did not understand them, the religious Romans and Anglicans, owned with armies respected during that time. Korea, Vietnam, the Gulf War, Afghanistan and Iraq are wars that were won or could have been won with the most powerful army known in the history of humanity, but at the end, thanks to the frightful foreign policy of "modern citizens", their international interventions not only resemble sovereign defeats but crowned the country with discredit and economic loss that was never recovered.

A nation that does not respect its history is and will be a bastard without lineage, an outcast without a country; such is the way the education system in the United States is educating new generations, so that the subject of history is considered, fraudulently, a thing of destiny, a nation which was formed to satisfy the needs of those without work or an honest way of living, a refugee for those who dream with having a pleasant way of life, their perverse mentors make them live inside the **ignorance** of their recent past, full of Glory and triumph that are hardly reached by **Rome or any other past empire.**

Another edge of social deterioration is that the falling of spiritually is double in its significance, motivated in part by the **brutal and dumb entrance of idolatry without control, and without establishing bases of rational tolerance, of course by respecting freedom of religion and freedom of choice, so that it is practiced in private by those who have these antagonistic inclinations to the followers of spiritual life in Christ in American land, pioneers discarded any confusion of "equality" for those who were their executors for many years.** This was consciously ignored by the "Pastor" Roger Williams, to justify his dastardly procedures and made himself be called the Champion of Liberty.

The rest of the decadency exists in the logic sequence of events, because if apostolic life decided to adopt pagan religious practices, full of idolatry, then, the pioneer spiritual life in America has been affected with the entering of denominations that have divided and weakened the body of Christ, which is considered the church, which has resulted in the daily fight against demons that occurs on the streets of the majority of the cities of the United States, and their indecent practices through television and internet, where crime, pain and love relations based on flesh and erotic beliefs are excused. This is all a complement of what was once the Christian life that the pioneers welcomed for the greatness and power of God our Lord Jesus Christ. That is the heavy rock load of guilt for the present citizens, which must be removed by them, in order to see the Glory of Our Lord Jesus Christ in the day to day living of this country. On the contrary and by continuing in this feast of flesh complacency, with sadness the warning that the God of Israel dictated to the Jeremias for Bharuch must be repeated:

"I WILL DESTROY WHAT I HAVE BUILT, AND RIP OFF WHAT I HAVE PLANTED, MEANING THAT I WILL OBLITERATE THIS EARTH AND THE LOOT AND FOR THOSE WHO ARE LEFT THEY MUST CONSERVE THEIR LIFE".

Let us give thanks to the Lord that the manifested revival in the congregations of the followers of Christ has awaken extinguished consciences where envisions of a new light of understanding exists motivated and created by the vivification of the Holy Spirit.

AMEN, AMEN AND AMEN.